CW00797085

SPIRIT OF
WEYMOUTH
and PORTLAND

ROGER HOLMAN

First published in Great Britain in 2009

Copyright text and photographs © 2009 Roger Holman

British Library Cataloguing-in-Publication Data
A CIP record for this title is available from the British Library

ISBN 978 1 906887 31 5

PiXZ Books
Halsgrove House, Ryelands Industrial Estate,
Bagley Road, Wellington, Somerset TA21 9PZ
Tel: 01823 653777
Fax: 01823 216796
email: sales@halsgrove.com

An imprint of Halstar Ltd, part of the Halsgrove group of companies
Information on all Halsgrove titles is available at: www.halsgrove.com

Printed and bound by Grafiche Flaminia, Italy

Weymouth

Prior to 1571 Weymouth consisted of two towns, Melcombe Regis on the northern side of the harbour and Weymouth on the southern side. They were always in contention over the profits of the haven between them, leading to poverty which followed protracted law suits. The Lords of the Council decided it was counter-productive to have two sea-board towns arguing while Spanish galleons were likely to appear at any time so they ordered the Bailiff of Weymouth and the Mayor of Melcombe to reconcile their differences and become one borough. This they did and with a contribution from the citizens of London, a bridge was built over the harbour in 1597 to symbolise their union.

Melcombe Regis goes down in history as the most likely location for the Black Death being introduced from the Continent into England, killing off a third of the population which in turn led to much social upheaval.

It is interesting to imagine what Weymouth would be like today if King George III had not been persuaded by a friend to visit the town in 1789. Fortunately for Weymouth he liked the place and continued to holiday there for another sixteen years, introducing other royalty, popularising sea bathing and bringing prosperity to the town.

Since 1995 when the Royal Navy vacated Portland Naval Base, Weymouth has had to rely more heavily on tourism by attracting new regeneration schemes. Being blessed with an above-average sunshine record, safe sandy beaches and the stunning backdrop of The World Heritage Jurassic Coast, it has become a very successful UK holiday destination.

The coming of the 2012 Sailing Olympics should boost the area's profile even more and have the benefit of a new road from Dorchester built to handle the increased traffic.

Roger Holman

Weymouth beach in summertime. The impressive Esplanade running the length of the bay, built between 1789 and 1805, was a direct result of royal patronage and the influx of summer visitors.

Above:
Mark Anderson made this sand sculpture of Windsor Castle for the Queen's visit in 2009.
He follows in the footsteps of his grandfather who was sand sculpting in 1925.

Opposite:
Seafront.

Queen Victoria's statue stands looking toward her grandfather, King George III's statue at the other end of the Esplanade.

King George's statue is guarded by a golden lion and a unicorn and is a much grander affair, erected by the grateful inhabitants of Weymouth. He never saw it because he stopped visiting the town a few years earlier. Seagulls are no respecters of persons even if they are royalty and find it an ideal resting place, although the council have given the King a head of spikes to deter them.

Lion and unicorn.

This bathing machine is now parked in the middle of a roundabout on the Esplanade but it was how the original bathers entered the sea, having had a horse pull the contraption into the water. When King George first ventured in to bathe, it was stated that he was in his birthday suit and the band struck up God save the King, which must have been reassuring for him! The town became popular but the mode of bathing did not.

13

Radipole RSPB Centre on the edge of the lake.

This is a rare transatlantic visitor, a Hooded Merganser seen at Radipole.

This is the old part of Weymouth with its narrow streets and in summer has a carnival atmosphere.

This cannonball still lodged in the wall
of a building located near the harbour
is a reminder of fierce battles that were
fought between the Royalists and the
Parliamentarians during the Civil War.

Left:
The Duke of Cornwall.

Right:
Weymouth's best-known landmark, known as The Jubilee Clock, was built in 1887 to mark the 50th year of Queen Victoria's reign. It has been the meeting place for generations of visitors and locals.

Every year Weymouth holds an international kite-flying festival.

Architecture that is typical of the Esplanade.

The land railway taking passengers the whole length of the Esplanade
and beyond to Lodmoor. It is another seafront attraction.

The lifting bridge which allows boats to pass out to sea from the inner harbour was opened by the then Duke of York in 1930.

Weymouth harbour, always bustling with activity populated with a variety of working ships, boats and pleasure craft.

The southern bank of the harbour is lined with charming early-nineteenth century houses.

Left:
A sailing boat in the harbour. In the days of sail one can imagine how impressive the harbour would have appeared full of such vessels.

Opposite:
Harbour.

Kelvin Moore, the skipper of this lobster fishing boat views his catch with a certain amount of respect.

A fierce looking gull stands guard.

One of the Brittany Ferries that sails
daily to the Channel Islands
and Cherbourg.

The inner harbour where most of the
pleasure craft are moored.

27

The harbour at dusk just prior to Christmas.

The Red Lion just off the harbour is in a pedestrian area, popular with visitors as a place to refresh, relax and soak up the atmosphere of the seaside town.

Opposite:
The Pier is really a walk on top of the harbour wall and because it is quite a long distance from the main beach, it probably doesn't get used as much as it deserves. A favourite place to fish, it allows magnificent views of the Jurassic Coast and Weymouth Esplanade.

Right:
Portland was one of the main manufacturing bases for torpedoes during the two World Wars. At its peak it employed over 1500 workers. Here Rodney Alcock, the now retired museum curator, explains the history.

Nothe Fort was completed in 1872 and its original guns were never fired in anger. In fact it is said that when they were test fired the vibration caused so much damage to the doors and windows, they had to be removed when firing took place. It was allowed to go to rack and ruin but has now been restored and is open and run by volunteers.

Nothe Fort showing what a commanding position it occupies.

Bowleaze Cove.

Isle of Portland from Green Hill.

Here are the only remains of a Roman Temple situated on the hill overlooking Bowleaze Cove. If the Romans returned today, what would they make of the nearby caravan development?

Overlooking Preston, which sits on the eastern edge of Weymouth and is connected to Sutton Poyntz.

Sutton Poyntz, a delightfully picturesque little village complete with duck pond snuggles contentedly under the nearby hills. Hardy's *Trumpet Major* is partly based on the village and the mill.

These are the beginnings of the new dual carriageway being built to relieve the congestion of the current road linking Dorchester to Weymouth and Portland. There was some opposition as there always is to new roads but the forthcoming Sailing Olympics at Portland probably proved the deciding factor.

King George III cut into the hill above Osmington Mills, riding away from Weymouth and perhaps the American colonies which were lost during his reign.

Portland

Portland is almost treeless and can be a very bleak place. It was described by Hardy as the Gibraltar of Wessex and he also named it 'Isle of Slingers'. It is scoured by centuries of stone quarrying and John Leland noted in 1540 "The people there be good in flinging of stones and use it for the defence of their Isle".

Although called an isle, in reality it is not, being tethered to the mainland by the narrow thread of Chesil Beach. Probably due to the inhabitants' isolation they developed and retained their own strange customs. They encouraged sex before marriage in case the union proved fruitless. They were also very superstitious; not daring to mention the word 'rabbit' for fear of bringing bad luck, probably due to the danger these little furry animals caused the quarrymen by burrowing.

The heyday for the industry was when a large quantity of the stone was used for the rebuilding of London after the Great Fire. Prince Albert laid the first stone of the breakwater in 1849 and it took over a quarter of a century to complete. It was fortunate that so much of the quarrying spoil was freely available but much of the hard work was performed by convict labour to which the locals were very much opposed. They soon realised there was a money-making potential to be exploited by transporting the visitors around the island to view the convicts at their labours.

Just off the Portland Beach Road within the harbour is a favourite location for board sailing and kite surfers. The big new development at Portland is just visible and high up on the hill is the Verne Citadel now Portland Prison.

The headquarters of the Sailing Academy.

Opposite:
The location of the Weymouth and Portland National Sailing Academy can be seen and where the 2012 Sailing Olympic and Paralympic Games will be held. The combination of clean winds, sheltered water and weak tides make this an unrivalled venue.

The new prestige housing development rising from the site of the old Naval station.

Portland Castle was another of the castles built by Henry VIII to protect Weymouth harbour when there was a fear of invasion from Catholic Europe. The only fighting the castle saw was during the Civil War when it changed hands several times.

Portland Castle from sea.

The Royal Naval cemetery
on Portland.

The Fleet is an 8-mile long part-freshwater, part-brackish lagoon which supports much wildlife. Barnes Wallis tested his prototype dambusting bouncing bombs on the Fleet.

The Swannery on the Fleet has the world's largest collection of swans that is open to the public. Swanherd David Wheeler resembles the pied piper at feeding time.

Opposite:
The entrance to the Fleet where it joins the harbour.

Right:
Dave Scott sorts through oysters that are farmed near the entrance to the Fleet. They are grown there for 3–4 years where the water rarely exceeds 23 degrees.

During rough weather the sound of the pebbles being thrown up on the bank and then dragged back by the surf is awe inspiring. Many ships have been lost along this stretch of the coast. Hardy named it Deadman's Bay.

The start of Chesil Beach at Portland.

Opposite:
Fortuneswell from
the beach.

Right:
Fortuneswell from
Portland Heights. The
houses are built on
the steep side of the hill
so one man's doorstep
can rise above his
neighbour's chimney.

Opposite:
The magnificent view of
Fortuneswell and Chesil.

Right:
Looking across the
harbour to Weymouth.

Left:
Chesil in rough weather.
The Beach stretches some
17 miles from Portland to
Burton Bradstock. It is an
awesome and unique
feature of the
Jurassic Coast.

Opposite:
Sunset over The Fleet
and Chesil.

At the top at Portland Heights stands an impressive statue of a stonemason backed by a fisherman representing the two main occupations of Portland workers over the years.

The Tout Quarry Nature Reserve and Sculpture Park. The spoils of quarrying have been put to good use here where Quarry Trust runs workshops teaching stone carving.

'Collage' of sculpturing in the Tout Quarry.

The spectacular cliff walk around Portland.

The church of St George Reforne stands isolated to the northwest of Easton.
It is a superb building built in 1754–66 by Thomas Gilbert, who strangely
does not to appear to have designed any other building.

Church Ope Cove is a tiny pebble cove accessed by a long flight of steps.

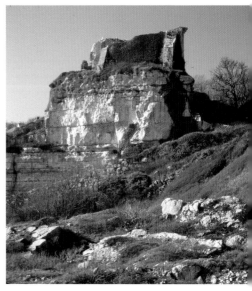

Rufus Castle or Bow and Arrow Castle overlooks Church Ope Cove and was built around 1300, but alas little survives today.

Portland Museum in the village of Easton.

The gardens in Easton.

Portland boast two lighthouses on Portland Bill. The smaller one was built in 1788 but is now used as a bird observatory. It was once the home of Dr Marie Stopes, the contraception pioneer.

The unmanned lighthouse, built in 1905, stands proud at a height of 135 feet dressed in a gown of red and white. Its very powerful light, is visible for some 18 miles and its sound in foggy weather can be quite startling if you are not expecting it.

The Pulpit Rock.

Rough weather at Portland Bill.